Samson and Delilah
My Two Loves

Elizabeth Rodenz

Samson and Delilah
My Two Loves
Copyright © 2022 by Elizabeth Rodenz
All rights reserved

This book is memoir. It reflects the author's present recollections of experiences over time. Some names have been changed. Some events have been compressed, and some dialogue has been recreated.

No part of this book may be reproduced or used in any manner without the prior written permission of the copyright owner, except for the use of brief quotations in a book review.

Elizabeth Rodenz
Pittsburgh, PA 15232
www.thedancingbridge.com

ISBN: 978-0-9722694-5-2 (hardcover)
ISBN: 978-0-9722694-4-5 (softcover)

Library of Congress Control Number: 2022904711
Samson and Delilah
A memoir by Elizabeth Rodenz
1. Dogs   2. Memoir   3. Dog Rescue   4. Dog Adoption
5. Pets

Preface

Dogs are forever. They are not to be tossed aside because they don't fit our version of a perfect dog. They kiss away our tears, cuddle next to us when we are sad, greet us with excitement and high spirits, even if we are in a bad mood, and stay by our side in times of trouble and tears. They know very well the meaning of the words, "till death do us part."

Wishing you as many blessings as there are stars and at least one dog in your future.

Elizabeth

To my husband, David, who embraced my love of dogs and encouraged me to write this book.

To Samson and Delilah who were by my side as I told their story.

To all of you who opened up your hearts to rescue a dog.

To those volunteers who work tirelessly with rescue groups.

Chapter 1
Unforgettable Day

A myth credits a mongrel dog with a crucial role in creation. Each day the first grandmother labored to weave a huge basket. If she finished the job, according to the myth, the world would suddenly end. Each night her little mutt diligently unraveled her hard day's work and thus saved humanity.
Unknown

Most of our days are forgettable. We do what we have to do or want to do. Along the way, we may laugh or cry, get angry, or be overjoyed. We also have memorable days that trigger events that bring us joy that lasts and lasts.

This is the story of that kind of unforgettable day for David and me—a day that would change our lives in innumerable ways.

The year David and I met, I lived in San Francisco, traveling back and forth across the country doing management workshops and coaching executives. He lived in New York City and was director of management training for a major communications company.

At times we actually found ourselves in the same city, some happenstance, some we planned. During one of those times, he asked me if I could do anything in my life, what would it be? I did not hesitate, "I want to write and have two dogs."

It had been too many years without a dog in my life. My work schedule and traveling had not permitted it.

He knew I wasn't much for sitting still, so he replied, "You can have that. You can climb any mountain, slay any dragon, do what you wish. The dogs and I will be waiting for you."

I smiled, thinking promises, promises.

Two years later…. After being away for ten years, I moved back to New York City and found an apartment on Central Park West.

Six months after my return, David and I began our search for two dogs by visiting the ASPCA on the city's East Side. I had told David and insisted, I guess, that we have to rescue dogs.

The first reason for rescuing was apparent to me but not enough to those who go out in search of a dog. We need to put puppy mills, pet stores, and fly-by-night breeders out of business.

Second, too many dogs are put to sleep, abused, abandoned, and in need of a good home. No argument from him. Of the two of us, I was the doggie person, having had dogs before, so he let me take the lead.

On a sunny day in June, we headed for the ASPCA on the East Side. On the bus, I sat, remembering when I had visited a shelter to adopt my first dog, and then the eight years spent as a volunteer with the ASPCA in San Francisco doing adoptions.

Walking through the door into the shelter, I said to David, "These places can be very sad."

An adoption counselor greeted us, and we explained that we wished to adopt two dogs.

"You can't adopt two dogs at the same time. If you prove to be a good owner to one dog, then you could adopt another."

We were surprised, but not disheartened. Maybe she would change her mind. Maybe we could get her to bend the rules, let us adopt two or.... Life is full of surprises.

In the room with wall-to-wall cages, tears welled up in my eyes as I looked into the faces of the dogs who were staring at us from behind bars.

I asked myself, should I ask to go inside the cage and pet and hug everyone or turn around and walk out? I had to persevere. We were there to save two dogs from continuing to live like this.

Some of the dogs were still as if frozen in time. Others lunged at the bars, pleading for a touch, a voice, some attention. Fortunately, not all the cages were filled with dogs, but I counted ten large dogs. No small ones.

Having volunteered in adoptions, I knew how difficult it is to get dogs adopted, especially in a city—landlords and co-op and condo boards being the challenge. Large dogs present another challenge.

The adoption counselor led us to a medium-sized dog down on all fours. She sighed and shook her head. "Her previous owner used a chain collar." She pointed to the scars around the dog's neck.

"As she grew older, it got tighter and tighter, and her skin grew around it. It had to be surgically removed. This deep scar remains."

"How could anyone do this to that sweet dog?" Anger was seething within.

"She has more than that scar. It may take her a long time before she trusts anyone again."

I walked over to her. There was no tail wag, no sign that she was aware of my presence. I knelt down and petted her head. No response. "She seems to be in shock," I muttered, trying to hold back my tears.

David turned to the counselor, "How long before we could adopt a second one?"

"I'm not sure. This one has bonded with another dog here. Maybe you'd like to see that dog?"

She brought in a large black and gray spotted dog.

"Oh, what a sweet face," I said as I touched her head and rubbed under her ears. Again, there was no tail wag or kisses or awareness of my presence.

"Both have been abused. Both dogs are going to take a lot of care. Maybe we could let you adopt both dogs, one after another. Neither will be ready for adoption for quite a while. Months probably. They need some training and socialization. You have plenty of time to think about it."

We left with me heartbroken. As we waited for the bus, I turned to David, "Why wouldn't they want someone to adopt two dogs?"

David shook his head, "Not all adopters are like you and had dogs before. So, how are we going to get two dogs? I'm sure all shelters have the same rules."

I chuckled, "We'll adopt one dog from one shelter and another dog from another. In fact, you can adopt one in your name, and I'll adopt one in mine."

My previously rescued dogs had taught me several lessons: Two dogs are easier than one; any dog is easy to love; age is just a number, not a disease. So, rescue!

Chapter 2

The Search is Over

If a man aspires towards a righteous life, his first act of abstinence is from injury to animals.
                    Albert Einstein

After our visit to the ASPCA, I was still determined to find two dogs that we could adopt either together or simultaneously, and I didn't want to wait months. Dogs were in shelters waiting for a home.

I decided to call the North Shore Animal League on Long Island. As I searched for the listing, I saw an advertisement for the CACC, Center for Animal Care and Control. I guess it was called the dog pound in days gone by. The ad stated that they had dogs for adoption.

A woman picked up the phone. I explained that we wanted to adopt two dogs at the same time. Oh my, I wished I had not said that. Not the same rule—one dog at a time!

"Is there a particular breed, size of dog you have in mind?"

"We don't care. Boxer, lab, mutt, or maybe beagles. I've had beagles before...."

"Beagles? Did you say beagles? We have two. They were just surrendered. We want them adopted together. You need to come right away. They'll be put down in 72 hours."

She spoke so quickly I wasn't sure I had heard her correctly. Two dogs, two beagles, both we could have at the same time. Could we be so lucky?

I confirmed all the information and promised we would come and see them the following day. David returned from his business trip that evening, and the following morning we trekked over to the East Side to the CACC.

A young girl came out from behind the counter. I explained that we were there for the beagles. She greeted us with a warm smile, "I'm glad you came so quickly."

"So, they haven't been adopted?"

"No, they're still here." She ushered us into what I would call a 'holding cell' for dogs. "The smaller one is a female, and the larger one is a male. They were surrendered together, so we want to keep them together."

She had already made that clear, but I guessed she was checking one more time to see if we still agreed to take both. Most people find one dog enough. I'm not one of them.

Amid the frenzied barking of a full house of dogs, two beagles were peering through the wires of their cage—the little one barking and the larger one howling. As we came near them, they stopped. I looked into their eyes and reached inside to touch them, to provide some comfort.

The male licked my hand as if saying, "Choose me. Oh, please choose me. I'm a nice dog."

The little one, the female, wiggled her bottom, her tail somewhat like a helicopter revving up as if saying, "I shouldn't be here. Get me out. NOW!"

"How old are they?" I said, getting in as much touching as possible, restricted by the wire cage between us.

"According to the previous owner, she's three, and he's two."

In order for us to meet them outside the cage, they were whisked away by someone to an area on the rooftop. When we got there, the male dog was racing around, jumping over the little female. She was barking at him as they raced in circles.

Once in a while, they stopped and gnawed on each other's ears or went mouth to mouth. We were bystanders and couldn't get in any pets or hugs. We couldn't help but smile and laugh at their antics.

I said to David after a few minutes. "He's so handsome, but look at how skinny he is."

We could see every rib in his body. His backside barely measured five inches across. His soulful eyes and the silly look on his face were riveting. I knew he would get adopted in time, but his time was going to be up on Monday or maybe Tuesday. It was then Saturday, and the CACC is closed on Sunday.

"She's also so thin," David said, going up to the female and rubbing behind her ears.

She had a skinny body atop long legs, not your short-legged stocky beagle. "It looks like she has had a litter recently. They probably used them for breeding," I sighed. "We'll never know what these dogs have been through."

After about five minutes of playtime, the female dog started barking and snapping at the male when he got too rough, calling a time out.

"Well, she's feisty. I like that about her and look at that curled-up tail."

David smiled and added, "He's playful, but why is he so much larger, and she's.... Is she really a pure-bred beagle?"

"She looks like one, but does it matter?"

I shared with David that years ago, I had found a dog book in the library that said that the American Standard Beagle was bred for longer legs than the short-legged chunky English beagle so they could run through the deep brush. The male looked like a perfect specimen. In fact, he looked like my last beagle, Autumn.

The smaller dogs are Elizabethan beagles. Queen Elizabeth I was reported to have had over one-hundred-fifty small beagles in the castle, so they named the petite lap dog beagle after her.

Within a few minutes, David said, "They're just perfect. Let's take them."

"I really would like two females." I paused. I guess I wanted more time to decide. Of the two of us, I could be called the procrastinator.

I looked over at the male dog. "We can't adopt her without taking him. What about the two female dogs at the ASPCA?"

David sighed. "This is a kill shelter, not like the ASPCA. These dogs only have a couple of days before they're put down if they can't get adopted. I guess we could take her and not him."

"They won't let us take one, and they're right about that. They should stay together." Someone opened the door to the rooftop, and the dogs were taken back to their cage. It was time for a decision.

Before I had my head wrapped around the idea of adopting these two dogs, David started the process. I hadn't had enough time with them to touch and hug and pet them, but deep down, I knew we were meant to be a family. Our search had ended.

As David filled in the forms, I asked the young woman why they were surrendered.

"I really don't know. People move and don't want to take them, or there's a divorce. We hear stories you could never imagine."

"So… what are their names?"

She checked the paperwork. "The male's name is Gordo. Her name is Negra."

I chuckled. "He's definitely not fat, and she's definitely tri-color. We're changing those names."

"So, we will spay and neuter them. That will all be done on Monday, and you can pick them up then."

We also agreed to micro-chipping, so if they got away from us somehow, there would be a record of us as owners.

Thinking about our travel schedules, I shouted out, "Oh my. We can't pick them up on Monday. I'm flying out tomorrow, coming back late Tuesday.

"David is leaving for a business trip on Tuesday. Our trips overlap. We can't leave them in the apartment alone.

I'm back late Tuesday. I can pick them up early Wednesday morning." So that was agreed.

We headed to the bus stop after they promised to keep them until Wednesday. While we waited for the bus along Second Avenue, David said, "So, are you excited… What's wrong? Do you want to change your mind?"

I was reminded of Autumn, a beagle I rescued from a shelter when I first lived in New York City. I remembered not wanting to adopt her because she did not look like my first beagle, Boomer.

Then I remembered how I believed I would never love Boomer as much as I had loved Snuffy, my first dog. In all instances, I was wrong. In all instances, I came to love them more than I could imagine.

I turned to David and said, "I can't wait until Wednesday."

When we got home, I wrote 'Beagles' on the calendar. It wasn't not because I would forget. I just wanted to mark the special date.

Chapter 3

What Joy!

Some of our greatest and historical national treasures we place with curators in museums; others we take for a walk.
Roger Caras

The following Monday, a woman from the shelter called David insisting that he come for the dogs. The female was spayed, the male was neutered, and they had to be picked up immediately. They were not willing to hold them until Wednesday as promised.

I was in Utah. David was leaving the following morning on his business trip. He sprang into action, so excited about having these two dogs in our home, and because that's David.

Weighing all the options, he ended up hiring a doggie taxi to pick up the dogs and take them to a veterinary clinic he found. The clinic would house them until I could pick them up.

I returned to New York Tuesday evening, and early on Wednesday morning, I made my way to the East Side to arrive early to collect the dogs. I paced back and forth, not sure how the dogs would react when they came through the door.

When they arrived, I realized they were more beautiful than I remembered. They greeted me with tail wags, and I delighted in petting and hugging their little bodies close to me.

The boy had luscious ears, long and soft and thick—a lovely handful. The little girl's ears were silky, and her black eyes captivating.

We were about thirty New York blocks from the apartment. That's over a mile—shorter if I cut through Central Park.

I was so excited about picking them up I did not think about how I would transport them home. The bus and the subway were not viable options—NO DOGS ALLOWED.

Executive car service was not an option, and the doggie taxi service didn't serve people. Neither was a New York taxi an option. It was difficult to get a taxi to pick you up with one dog, let alone two.

I checked out their spaying and neutering stitches, and they looked fine. I decided to walk them home, so off we went. We would stroll and take many breaks and, once in a while, flag a taxi just in case the driver liked dogs or needed the money.

It surprised me that they were not pulling on the leads. They were probably shocked by the hustle and bustle of the New York streets. People coming at them, shouting, honking horns.

As we passed people along the way I smiled and chuckled watching the dogs' tails wagging. After walking about thirty or forty minutes, we entered Central Park at Fifth Avenue and 59th Street.

I found a bench where we could take a break. People of all ages, some with their children, came up to pet the dogs and visit, many telling me how cute they were.

A constant question was: What are their names? I explained they were just adopted so I got advice and suggestions for names and care, the shots they would need, and so on.

I spoke to more people that day in New York than I had in the previous six months I had lived there.

We turned the corner, and the boathouse was in sight. The male's attention was immediately riveted by the smell of hot dog vendors. I sweet-talked him away with pets and cooing.

We walked past the carousel, the music playing, the children squealing, and when we turned a corner, a horse and buggy were approaching.

The female dog let out loud barks that pierced everyone's eardrums within six New York blocks. The male dog started to howl non-stop, stopping passersby in their tracks, many smiling and laughing at the sight of two little dogs challenging a big horse and carriage.

I couldn't help but laugh and eventually coaxed them away. We walked towards the bridge near the West Side and into the Brambles. The two little dogs were hoovering along, sniffing every tree and piece of paper.

Once in a while, they chased a squirrel up a tree, thrilled with the adventure. After several hours of pets and visits with strangers, we were home.

A section of our apartment had ample open space of about a thousand square feet with twelve-foot ceilings.

The dogs looked like miniature furniture in such a vast space.

Immediately, the female dog started sniffing around, checking every nook and cranny. Seemingly content in her new home, she settled on the bed I had made with pillows and blankets. She watched my every move with her black eyes.

The male dog followed me everywhere. Every time I turned around, he was there, and I frequently found myself tripping over him.

That evening I fed them, and then we walked across the street into Central Park. The first thing I noticed was that the male dog did not lift his leg. He squatted just like the female. How funny, but I must admit I preferred that he squatted.

The two dogs raced around at hyper speed on their extension leads, sniffing the lamp poles and the ground and once more chasing squirrels up the trees.

From the first time I lived in New York City in the '80s, Central Park had been my haven of contentment. There is no place I would rather be than in New York, and it was made all the better because of those two beagles.

That night I realized that my life was filled with the warmth and cuddles of two dogs. They were bringing light back into my life—the light that went out when my father had passed away seven months before.

That night David called from Burbank. My first words were, "Guess what? The boy squats just like the girl. No leg lifting."

I must admit that was one of my concerns about the male—lifting his leg against the furniture. We laughed, and then I told him of our adventures in the park and that they were cuddled in the bed beside me.

He chuckled, "Well, spoiling them didn't take long. We're going to have to talk about where they sleep when I get home."

"D'you remember saying, 'We won't need a queen bed?' Well, you may change your mind."

Looking down at the two dogs snuggling beside me, I found I was falling in love. The male had eyes that reached into my soul and an impish look that tugged at my heart.

The female…well…It was hard to explain, but there was something about her I could not identify yet. Whatever it was, it had cemented us together. We were rescuing them, but I also knew they were rescuing me.

The following morning the male dog followed me into the bathroom, sat on the rug, and when I stepped out of the shower, he started licking me. He was so gorgeous and gentle. I almost cried at the attention he was bestowing upon me. I quickly dressed, fed them, and rushed out the door for our visit to the park. I had landed in heaven.

Since there was no kitchen door, David had bought a baby gate so we could restrict the dogs to the kitchen when I had to go out. The male could leap the gate in a single bound.

Everything I put in his way, he jumped over. Nothing was going to keep him from being by my side. There was an umbilical cord between the two of us, and all evidence told me he was not going to sever it any time soon, if ever.

Not convinced that the dogs were house-trained, I could not allow them the freedom of the apartment when I left that evening. I had promised to attend a meeting that I shouldn't miss.

I thought of sequestering them in the bathroom, but they might have scratched the door, torn it apart, or barked to be free, disturbing the neighbors.

Believing the male dog would be a challenge to keep in place, I put a twelve-foot stepladder in the entry. We had bought it to change light bulbs and hang pictures high up. Remember, we had twelve-foot ceilings.

I added chairs, the ironing board, suitcases, and boxes, everything I could find until the items reached up at least five feet. When I had finished stacking these items, I laughed at the sculpture I had created. "That should hold him," I said under my breath.

As I closed the apartment door and pressed the elevator button, the male was howling. That howling could not continue. I wasn't sure how tolerant the neighbors would be. I unlocked the apartment door and tried to settle him down.

I thought having the little girl with him would keep him calm, but that didn't work either. They were both tugging at my heart. I wanted to stay and spend time with them. They were bringing me such joy, but I needed to be at this meeting.

Once the male was quiet, I left a second time. He started howling again, so I waited at the elevator door until he stopped. I was not sure if he would howl again, but then we were in a New York City apartment, so I believed I would know in time if he did.

Throughout the entire evening, my thoughts were back in the apartment with my two little dogs. When the meeting ended, I rush out and raced home. I opened the apartment door. The male dog was in the hallway and greeted me with enthusiasm. I looked around for the little girl but couldn't find her.

I peered through the ladder and boxes and suitcases and saw her sweet face and her wagging tail. As I moved the debris away to rescue her, I couldn't see any evidence that the boxes and suitcases had been moved. Apparently, the male had climbed up the ladder and jumped down. It's a miracle he hadn't damaged a body part doing that.

As I lay awake that night, I realized I should not have left them. It was too soon to abandon them. It was then I knew that this loveable male dog with that gorgeous face was going to be a challenge. I hoped I would be up for it.

Chapter 4
A Tug of Wills

He is your friend, your partner, your defender, your dog. You are his life, his love, his leader. He will be yours, faithful and true, to the last beat of his heart. You owe it to him to be worthy of such devotion.
Unknown

"The boy chewed the chair leg," I cried into the phone. "He's two. I thought he'd grown out of his puppy stage."

David, attempting to be helpful, said, "I guess we need to get him some toys."

David was still in Burbank and called several times a day, always looking forward to stories about the dogs. These were either tales of Samson's capers that were testing my patience or ones of delight about their antics that had made me laugh.

When David returned from his business trip, we started enjoying the dogs together. When we had been looking for an apartment, it had been essential to find a place close to Central Park because I knew there were going to be dogs in our future. That ended up to be a good call.

On the weekends, we got up early, grabbed some breakfast, fed the dogs, and raced to Central Park across the street. I'm not sure who was more excited about those outings—the dogs or David and me.

Once in the park, we met passersby who petted the dogs and chatted about the lovely day. The dogs took in the world around them. They were good teachers.

These precious dogs had not only latched on to our hearts, but they had immersed us in their world. They showed us how to relax, exercise, ignore work issues, and how to spend our time laughing, forgetting about everything but being together.

After moving into our apartment six months earlier, we had gone in search of a new mattress. We decided we would get a full-size bed. Neither of us is tall or large, and space in our apartment was at a premium, so it was the obvious choice.

We hadn't factored in two dogs. When the little beagles—still no names--jumped in with us, the bed shrank, and we found ourselves on the very edges, especially me, because they were usually cuddled on my side.

Each night, David snuggled them down into their bed on my side on the floor. I looked down at their sweet faces, wanting to sweep them up in my arms and put them in bed, but I resisted. David believed they would disturb our sleep and was adamant that the dogs should stay on their bed.

Night after night, one of us woke up to find the boy snuggled between us. If David woke, he put the boy on his bed. If I found him there, I was unwilling to remove him. Wanting the little girl to have the same privilege, I put her in the bed beside me.

I loved snuggling both dogs. They usually slept quietly, not disturbing us, but David kept persevering with the bed on the floor. I say "the boy" because the girl came with a halo. She stayed where she was put. It was clear, both the male dog and David were determined. Who was going to win the tug of wills?

Their second weekend with us, we decided to take a trip to visit my mother, who was then spending many of her days alone in the house, unable to drive for the last ten years. I was always in two minds—wanting to see my mother and missing my father. My father and I had had a special bond that went deeper than words, and I missed him every day.

My mother was a dear friend and a loving mother. She understood my wanderlust, my inner strength. She had inspired me over the years, starting when I had been about ten, by saying, "Elizabeth, you can do whatever you want." I had been blessed with two caring parents, both special in my life. After losing my father, I found myself clinging to our memories.

We had driven my ten-year-old Mazda M6 to New York from San Francisco the year before, so we had wheels in the city—a rarity. I put a blanket and pillows in the back seat for the dogs and once the car started moving, the boy buried himself under the blanket.

The girl stood up on the armrest, her eyes darting all around and her nose twitching, taking in all the sensory information she could.

After they had settled, the girl decided she liked the view from the console. That's when we started to call her our co-pilot. After about ten minutes, she pushed her way into the front seat.

I complied without hesitation. I grabbed her pillow and put it on my lap so she would be comfortable, and I wouldn't have her bony body pushing into mine.

"Are you sure you want her to sit on your lap for the next three hundred miles?" David said, already knowing the answer.

"She's so cute, and yes, I love having her cuddling next to me."

Realizing that his sister was getting attention and he was not, the male threw the blanket off and started to make his way forward. He had his front paws on the console between the two seats and his back paws on the back seat.

"Where do you think you're going, good boy?" I laughed, reaching to rub him under his ears.

David looked over at him. "Well, he can't ride the entire way straddling the console and back seat."

"I think he's stubborn enough to do so." He then jumped into the front seat squashing his sister and me. Without hesitation, I grabbed the second pillow and put it on the console to rest his bony body. That made it difficult for David to shift gears, but it was clear that David had to adjust, not our sweet boy.

When we arrived at my mother's home, she greeted us all with enthusiasm. She wasn't the besotted dog lover that my father had been, but she was always kind and caring to all the dogs in the family and those who had come under her care.

The obvious question from my mother and other family members was: "What are their names?" We knew we had to name them, but we had decided to wait until they had been with us for a while—thinking their names would come to us.

A few days after we had adopted them, I had suggested Bagel and Biscuit. David had asked which one would we call Bagel? It was clear that although those names were cute, they just didn't seem to fit.

I mentioned to my family that I had named my last rescue dog Autumn because I got her in October and her brown color was like the rust fall leaves. My niece suggested naming the female Summer because we got them in July. So, what do we call the male? A nephew suggested Sammy.

That's when it hit me somehow. Let's name the male Samson and the female Delilah. They were perfect names for these two loves. The male was gorgeous with an extraordinary face and lean body, and I knew he would be a muscular dog once he gained some weight—a perfect Samson. The female had bewitching ways with beautiful black eyes—a gorgeous Delilah.

We cuddled them to us, and I cooed "Handsome Samson" and "Delightful Delilah."

Chapter 5

Just Samson Please!

Every new dog who comes into my life gifts me with a piece of their heart. If I live long enough, all the components of my heart will be dog, and I will become as generous and loving as they are.

Unknown

David is an early riser, and because he had fallen so hard for our two loves, he wanted to spend as much time with them as possible. Even before they arrived in our home, he announced that he wanted to walk them before he left for work, getting up a half-hour earlier to do so.

Every morning Samson bounced out of bed, tail wagging, prancing around, ready to start the day with David. Delilah's big eyes opened, and she let out a loud sigh as David rousted her teeny body from her sleepy state next to me.

I agreed with her. I was for staying put—not a morning person since I had started my own business. I had never heard a dog sigh before and with such emphasis. Their antics started our day with smiles and often laughter.

The dogs became quite comfortable with the morning ritual, even though Delilah continued to sigh and grumble at being awakened. Depending on our travels, I would walk them later in the day, and David and I both walked them after dinner.

As we walked along, I started to sing, "I love you a bushel and a peck, a bushel and a peck and a hug around the neck."

Their tails wagged, and they looked back at us. Also, to get them to walk with calm, I would say, "March it out. One-two, one-two, one-two."

I thought it was crucial that the dogs should hear my voice so they would know we were right there with them. It made me smile and often chuckle to watch them strut out along as though they were indeed marching

Within seconds of entering the park, Samson and Delilah made sure the squirrels returned up the trees, and Samson especially greeted every dog that appeared friendly. Delilah usually ignored other dogs, content to be on her own.

Heading north in the park took us around a large pond with ducks. Sometimes an egret would dive into the water. Samson would often chase the ducks but knew to stop short of going into the water.

We seldom saw people and their dogs a second or third time. I guess because we always headed in a different direction—either to the East Side around the pond or somewhat south and west toward the carousel. Every day was a different adventure.

I often heard comments that a particular dog was owned by a celebrity living off or near Central Park. We didn't pay much attention. They're entitled to their own time with their dog, just doing a job like everyone else, and having a dog like the rest of us.

Both Samson and Delilah pulled so hard when they saw a squirrel or another dog. My arms started to ache, waking me at night and often keeping me awake.

Around that time, we took Samson and Delilah to the vet for a checkup. He suggested a leader collar for them which would make it easier to walk and control their movement. It would minimize their chances of having arthritis in the neck and back when they got older.

He said, "Imagine having your neck yanked every time you take off in a hurry. The same would happen with a dog's back if you used a harness. The neck and back get ripped every time."

He reached for a pamphlet. "It's not a collar. It looks something like a horse's bit. Don't let that turn you off. It's a kinder and gentler way to walk them. You direct and redirect them by simply pulling on the lead. That strap tugs at the nose and moves the head in the direction you wish. It will calm them, especially the male who appears high energy."

He gave us a card with a woman's name and telephone number. We called her, and the next day she arrived with several leads of different sizes. She pulled out a red one that she thought would fit Samson.

"It slips over the nose and then under the chin and behind the ears. The strap clips at the top of the neck. The goal is to limit dog injuries, as well as calm a dog."

Samson nudges her to pet him. "How does it calm a dog?"

"When a female dog wants to calm her pups, she puts her mouth around their muzzles. When we want to calm our dogs down, we rub them behind their ears and under their chin. The straps touch those parts of their head and have the same calming result."

"It looks like a muzzle," David said.

"Some people may think so, but the dog can still eat, bark, lick."

She then fitted Delilah with a turquoise blue one—the only small size she had. She had some liver treats with her and held one out as she slipped the collar over Samson's nose. She did the same with Delilah.

"Use a treat at the beginning to get it on. Eventually, the dogs will probably just accept it. Let's take them for a walk."

We got on the elevator and took them into the park. It was incredible how easy it was to pull the dogs in a particular direction. And it was easy to hold them back without putting strain on my arms and neck.

We were hooked, and Samson and Delilah didn't seem to mind, although Samson stopped and pawed at it every so often. Delilah never bothered. As I said, she had a halo over her sweet head.

We noticed on our outings that passersby would stare at the dogs. Some would do their best to walk as far around and away from us as they could.

Other times children who wanted to pet the dogs were cautioned not to do so, with comments such as "That dog may bite you." "I don't think those dogs are friendly." "They're wearing muzzles—be careful."

We had to admit those comments surprised us since those thin strips across the nose in red and blue definitely did not resemble a muzzle. Time and time again, when we had an opportunity, one of us would explain that it was not a muzzle, the dogs would not bite, and they could still eat and drink. The collar was kinder to dogs than a harness or neck collar.

Other times people told us they had tried it, but their dog didn't like it and pawed at its nose. One of us would then explain, "Dogs don't like any collar, any harness. They want to run free. If they could get their paw back to their neck or their back, they would try to get that collar or harness off too."

That comment often surprised people because they had never thought about what a dog must feel with a collar around her neck or a harness around his body.

"You have to ask yourself who's in charge," David would often say.

Then sometimes I might add, as I looked down at Samson and Delilah, who seemed to want to get a bark in, "Our dogs can't decide what's best for them. We have to do that. As you can see, they get used to it. Yes, you may abandon it again but give it a second chance."

We don't know how many people we'll get to think about their decision to use a neck collar or any kind of harness. Still, our goal is to give them something else to consider.

Chapter 6
Tabula Rasa

I liked the idea of adopting a dog beyond the puppy stage, a dog with an unknown span of life under his belt. It seemed only fair; he didn't know what he was getting into with me either.
Meg Donohue

Every few hours during the day, Samson picked up a teddy bear or one of his other toys and shook it in Delilah's face. Delilah abandoned her perch, grabbed a toy, and raced around the room. This was their way of announcing "playtime."

Dogs have a way of capturing delight at the moment. They experience that moment to the fullest, in the present. Playing with Samson or watching him and Delilah play together made me smile, and they never failed to bring joy and delight to my life. That laughter released tension and stress and renewed my spirit. Play gave me a chance to be silly, talk in a funny voice, and immerse myself in their world of play.

When I told them we were going out, they danced around me and chased each other with unrestrained enthusiasm, celebrating their good fortune. Through spending time together and playing, bonds were forged, and the more any of us engage in play, the deeper the bonds.

Samson and Delilah also reminded me how natural and essential play and laughter were to my well-being. Their paw prints were quickly being stamped on my heart day after day.

There are no words to describe the joy Samson and Delilah were bringing into our lives. Two little dogs surrounded us with so much pleasure and joy, so, of course, I wanted to share our good news.

A few weeks after adopting Samson and Delilah I was telling a long-time acquaintance about our new family members. Thinking she would be delighted for us, I was surprised when she said, *"I only get kittens. Then I can raise them the way I want."*

I could not be mute. "Then why do so many people raise puppies and kittens that don't turn out the way they wanted and they end up in shelters?"

Her silence was loud, so I continued, "Yes, we're having our struggles…."

"But you could have gotten puppies."

"Their lives were on the line. Someone needs to rescue the thousands of dogs in shelters. Yes, we could have gotten puppies, but there are lots of people wanting puppies."

"Why were they surrendered? What do you know about their previous owners?"

"Nothing, so we need to figure out what to do. Now they're ours, and these two precious dogs need to be loved and cared for." Whew! That felt good.

I told David what she said and added, "She believes that adult dogs and cats are broken and need to be fixed. She thinks that kittens and puppies come with a clean slate—tabula rasa."

"You sound angry."

"I guess I am. What if everyone had that attitude? Dogs and cats would live out their lives in shelters or be put down. Yes, there could be problems..."

David nodded and chimed in, "Besides, puppies and kittens don't come with a guarantee either."

I chuckled, "Or a how-to guide, but given the way most are written, it wouldn't matter. Besides, puppies don't grow up quickly. There are different struggles. Time and effort are required no matter whether the dog is a puppy or not."

David stood there and looked at me.

"Yes, I know. I'm ranting."

"No, no. I agree. They are definitely not blank slates, so what do you want to do?"

"They deserve a chance. We cannot toss them aside because they made mistakes. I guess we have to be patient and believe in them."

"I think we are and do."

"Well, you're more patient than me because you don't spend as much time with them as I do, but what to do is still a *puzzlement*."

In my quiet moments, I came to realize that I wanted Samson and Delilah to be dogs. I did not want to make them accept standards of behavior and do tricks—behavior and tricks we never would ask of a cat or a cow or a duck. Only dogs seem to be told what to do and when to do it.

I did not want to squash their spirit, their uniqueness, but we needed them to change their behavior so we could all live happily in a New York City apartment. Eventually, I wanted them to do what was needed not because I commanded them to do so but because it was normal behavior.

Dogs, like all of us, run on their own time clocks, and David and I could not have unrealistic expectations about how long it would take them to mend their ways. especially Samson. How long should it be, I was not sure, but I was committed to giving them that time.

Delilah, *the girl with the curl* (in her tail, that was), spent most of her days in the quiet comfort of her bed unless she was romping with Samson or we took a walk. Samson was the opposite. He would roam the apartment and enjoyed running around, barking, and biting Delilah's back legs when she joined him in play.

He jumped on the furniture and chewed anything in sight. He would still howl, especially when left, and his howl was so loud that I was sure it could be heard many blocks away.

When Samson howled or barked, I did what was expedient at the time. I shouted, "Samson, shut up," and quickly moved towards him. Despite being a loving and precious dog, I raised my voice to stop him from chewing a table leg or barking, or getting into some kind of trouble, but he paid little attention.

My agitated state and loud voice did not stop him, and at times animated him. It didn't matter that my nerves were on edge because there was a New York Board, and people in the building hadn't been that friendly. He was a dog and didn't feel my pain.

I noticed, though, when I raised my voice, Delilah rolled over on her back, asking to be petted. When I asked Samson to go to his bed, Delilah complied. Samson did not. Samson was going to do what he wanted to do. My behavior spoke volumes to both.

Horrified that I was scaring Delilah when I yelled and frustrated that Samson would not do what I asked of him, I decided I must change my tactics with Samson. I had to change MYSELF to change Samson's behavior, but what was I to change myself into?

Of course, I had to stop because I realized Samson was saying, "Yelling doesn't stop me," and Delilah was telling me, "I'm a good girl," or maybe, "Yelling is scary." That thought upset me as well. I didn't want her to be frightened in any way.

I decided I must pay attention to what they were telling me. When I called Delilah, she came running and danced around me with delight. I jokingly said to David, "She loves her name. That's why she comes running, her tail wagging." I believed it was actually the sound of my voice, the way I said her name.

On the other hand, Samson ignored me when I called him to come, even though he followed me everywhere.

"How did we get a dog with no ears?" I said, chuckling. Then the reality hit me. When I was upset, I spoke his name in a loud voice.

I said Delilah's name in a soft, gentle, and sometimes lively voice. Delilah associated her name with something good, while Samson did not.

Samson was saying that a booming voice would not change his behavior, so I had to rethink what I was doing. Intellectually, I knew not to yell, but in the heat of the moment, I just couldn't always stop. I had work to do.

Chapter 7
Tilted Halos

My goal in life is to be as good a person as my dog already thinks I am.
Paul Dunn

Every day people become guardians to dogs for various reasons. Duke was brought home because he is handsome and will be fun to take on runs. Maggie is cute and will make a good playmate for the kids. Then the reality of having a dog becomes known.

Later, people drop them off at shelters, telling themselves it's for the best. Others drop them off along a road or on a doorstep. There is no reason for such inhumane treatment. They are just dogs, and they won't mind being cast aside. Right? Wrong!

Some people don't want to spend the time and effort it sometimes takes to train a dog. Most often, though, it's because they don't know what to do.

The belief, "You're a dog. I'm your owner. You should obey," would be funny if it didn't result in so many problems and in times such sadness.

Living in an apartment in New York City with a howling beagle is a new experience. David and I talked about it repeatedly, and eventually, he suggested a dog trainer. We could not give up on Samson, or abandon him as his first owners had done.

"Well, I could at least talk to one and get an idea of what they do, but I don't think that's the answer. It's up to us. One size doesn't fit all."

"You're wearing your management hat."

"Well, the challenges I face remind me of the challenges managers face."

"Like what!"

"Well, you don't manage one person at a time. The same with the dogs. Samson's soulful eyes follow me when I pet or speak to Delilah. Delilah's big eyes peer out from under the blanket when she hears me playing or talking with Samson. They notice everything I do with the other. Their eyes follow me when I'm near, and they are interested in every move I make."

"Well, you're the center of their world."

"Yes, I know it sounds funny, but I believe they know when one is being treated better than the other."

David chuckled, "Well, I don't know about better, but I'm sure they know when one is getting something the other isn't. See what a trainer has to say."

The following day I called a trainer. After I heard the amount he charged, I caught my breath and asked, "What guarantee that the dog would be trained."

"What's the breed?"

"Beagle."

"Beagle. No guarantee. They're stubborn and difficult to train."

"I have had beagles before, and they are wonderful dogs."

I thanked him for his time and banged down the phone. The trainer was starting with the belief that he would fail, and he had a built-in excuse if indeed he did — the dog's breed. I also realized that sending a dog to be trained is a quick-fix. The dog is being put into the hands of another, so we wouldn't have to do anything. No, no, no!

Then I realized that David and I had to figure out what to do. There was no quick fix. There was no template. Every dog is different. Samson and Delilah were talking to us every day, and they were telling us what worked and what did not. We just had to pay attention and listen.

In reality, it was obvious that we needed to be trained. It was our end of the lead that was faulty. We needed training. We also had to be committed to them, although that would not stop us from making mistakes.

We had to keep trying to work things out, so we could all live happy lives. I believed, as Samson and Delilah would soon prove, old dogs can learn new tricks and so could we.

We were heartened by the improvements we were seeing, but we were disheartened because it was taking so long. During that time, there was always the ever-present concern of our neighbors and the co-op board.

The owner of the apartment next door was not at all neighborly, so he was a definite concern. We rarely saw him. One day I knocked on his door to deliver a package that had been wrongly delivered. I did not ask about the dogs, and he did not say anything. I thought he might complain or maybe he had already, and the thought of selling and trying to find another place to live was frightening.

Finding this home had taken us six months. The other choice was to give Samson up. Neither choice was acceptable.

One decision we made was to get a crate, so when we went out, Samson could not chew anything. We wanted him to be comfortable, so we got a large one, which dominated our living space.

During the day, I would throw a toy inside the crate to get him to go in. He had water and more toys inside, including a pillow and blanket. If he started to chew something, not his, I would get him inside the crate with something he is allowed to chew.

Once in a while, we asked Delilah to join him—not because she was a problem but just to keep him company. After a few weeks, the crate became like a piece of furniture.

When Samson was chewing something that was not his, all I had to do was look at him. He went in the crate on his own and stayed there until I called him out. He was just so adorable I couldn't help but chuckle.

After a time, he just went in the crate because. "Good Samson Boy."

Chapter 8
Hey Diddle Diddle

Rescue is not just a verb. It's a promise.
Unknown

"Hey, Diddle, Diddle, Cat and the Fiddle. The cow jumped over the moon. Little doggie laughed to see such fun. Because the dish ran away with the spoon." This is the song I sang to Delilah.

One of the nicknames I gave her was "Diddle Dee." When she heard my voice or greeted me, just like the first time I saw her in that cage, her whole body started to wiggle, so another nickname was born—"Wiggle Bottom."

Dogs spend their days watching our every move, what we do, and never assigning any motive to our behavior. They have a better understanding of our behavior and quirks than we do of theirs.

They are masters of their masters. Think how often your dog convinced you to give her a treat or pet him. Think of how much time you spend walking them in the rain and snow. Think about all you do for your dog, *just because*.

Although they were both beagles, Samson and Delilah were different in more than just their gender. Samson's name was perfect for him—not only was he muscular, but he was also strong-willed, proud, and with a sense of purpose. He liked to cuddle but was also playful and curious with high energy.

Samson would race around the apartment, stopping now and then to investigate whatever was in his path. He was trying to find something to keep himself entertained. Often it was a furniture leg, a cushion, a magazine, whatever he could have fun gnawing or shredding.

One day I shared with David what I had been thinking for weeks. "I realize that it's easy to be Delilah's Mom. She's not destructive and is quiet most of the time. Being Samson's Mom isn't that easy."

I must admit I just loved his playfulness and energy. He was just so darn cute, but I couldn't have him destroy the furniture and continue to howl. So, what to do? I needed to relax, breathe, and change my mind set about his behavior.

I began by thinking of him as a curious dog that needed to amuse himself and I appreciated his joyfulness and enthusiasm. The change in my attitude triggered new responses and behaviors on my part.

I stopped yelling and called him to me in a soft voice. I gave him positive attention—petting and hugging him when he appeared. I praised him repeatedly--every time he did something that I wanted him to do. I clapped my hands and called him to me, rubbing his ears and cooing, "Good Samson Boy."

When I wanted to stop him from doing something he shouldn't do I redirected his behavior. I told him to do something that I knew he enjoyed, such as, "Samson, bring me a toy." He raced to get the toy, dropping whatever he was doing.

Telling him to do something more fun and exciting, rather than trying to stop him from doing something destructive, minimized his getting into trouble. I praised him for good behavior every chance I got, and since he loved hugs and pets and cuddles, he was more than happy to do what I asked.

I also spent time teaching them both something new. Samson loved to be by my side while I taught them to sit, come, stay, or get down—commands that could save their lives if they were nearing danger. Teaching them something was another form of good attention, and praise and pets were an added bonus.

My heart was light when Samson's face tilted to one side, and Delilah's curly tail wagged at the sound of my voice. I told them they were good doggies in a playful voice, sometimes several times a day but definitely every day.

It made me feel good to make them feel good—to see Samson dance around Delilah and me while she wiggled her bottom with delight. We were their world, and they had become an important part of ours. What bliss!

I believe there is no such thing as a bad dog. Some dogs do bad things, things that make us angry. One thing that became clear to me was that I had to take responsibility for Samson's behavior.

If he chewed a pillow, I needed to make sure it was not there to tempt him. If the stuffing got in his throat, he could have choked and possibly died. He did not know the danger when he started chewing, but I did.

It wasn't only a matter of the damage, but the harm that could come to him if he got stuffing stuck in his throat, cutting off his breath, or lodging in his intestines, or a piece of wood landed in his lung.

I don't find any humor when a dog gets into this kind of trouble. The horrors are too many to think about. The dangers are too great to be funny. That is why it is imperative to take the time to train our dogs, remove all obstacles that can harm them, and show affection. Not because we want to control their every move, but because we ask them to live in a world where there are dangers they cannot comprehend.

Samson was signaling that he was a high-energy dog. There was just not enough for him to do. He also needed direction, attention, and praise and was more than happy to learn something new. I knew at my gut level that he was a beautiful dog, kind and gentle and loving.

Chapter 9

Samson is Bored

Dogs have a way of finding people who need them, filling an emptiness we didn't even know we had.
                    Thom Jones, American Writer

Samson and Delilah danced around us, sniffing our clothes as we got dressed each morning.

I said to David. "The dog knows whether they are going for a walk or we are leaving them at home."

David looked at me, puzzled.

I chuckled. "They know by the clothes we wear."

If we put on 'Mommy-and-Daddy-are-going-out' clothes, they snuggle down on their beds. If they are 'We're-going-for-a-walk' clothes, they race around the apartment, summoning us, the members of their pack, to get moving.

When I told my mother about Samson's antics, she said, "Elizabeth, he's bored."

Bored! Maybe more toys would be the answer—something Samson was allowed to chew. So, we went in search of toys of every shape and size.

Once we had a collection, Samson left the furniture alone. I would find him chewing one of his toys or tossing it up in the air and trying to catch it. Over the next month, we added more.

I started a ritual of rotating the toys. It was driven by the fact that some toys needed washing and others had to be mended. The washed ones we tucked away and brought them out again later.

I did this every week or two. By recycling Samson's old toys and adding new ones now and then, he was continually getting a different toy, or so Samson thought. His nickname soon became "toy boy."

We also bought toys with a squeak in them and encouraged everyone else to do the same, so I could separate play from trouble. When I heard the squeak, I knew Samson was chewing his toys, not the furniture. I also put a bell on his collar, so I could hear where he was and find him more easily.

The toys also provided us an opportunity to exercise him. One of us would throw the toy across the room, and he would go get it and come running back to us, pleased with himself and begging us to keep playing. Often, he would not drop it, so then we played tug of war.

We played "dog in the middle." David stood on one side of the room, and I was at the other end. I threw the toy to David, and Samson ran to him to get it. David would catch it or let it fall to the ground but grabbed it before Samson did. He then threw it back to me, with

Samson chasing after it. We did this until one of us got tired, but it was never Samson.

Delilah also loved to play with soft toys, so we bought smaller ones for her. She would pick up a toy and shake it back and forth so hard it seemed her head would fall off.

Samson and Delilah were teaching us to pay attention to what they told us. We just had to be willing to listen and learn.

Samson was teaching us that a soft, purring voice got his attention. When he was on his bed without being told to do so, I petted his head or scratched behind his ears and said in a soft, purring voice, "*Good Samson boy.*" Then butter would not melt in his mouth—he seemed so innocent, and his adorable little horns (I have come to love them) were invisible.

Howling was a different problem we had to curb. Dogs naturally bark, and beagles—well, some of them—naturally howl. I had never heard a louder howl than Samson's, so what to do? When would he stop?

When Samson was howling, the thought of being asked by the co-op Board to give up the dogs or sell the apartment put me on edge most of the time.

It was not more than a month before the Board wrote me a letter complaining about the dogs and asking us to correct the problem. We had to do something, but we were doing everything we could and knew how to do it. We believed they had settled down a lot, especially

Samson, who had a long way to go from the beginning. It was just going to take a little longer.

I wrote the Board explaining what steps we had taken in detail. Would our efforts be enough? Would the quiet that existed most of the time be sufficient to please our neighbors and silence the Board?

Walking to the Brambles, watching the carousel and listening to the music, trudging through the deep snow, I came to realize that all these everyday trips were gifts—gifts that the dogs were giving us, gifts we should appreciate and value, for we might never pass that way again.

One day I walked the dogs to the East Side of the Park. As we made our way down a steep slope, I slipped on the wet grass, and my butt landed hard on the granite rocks behind me. I cried out, but fortunately still had hold of the dogs' leads.

As tears ran down my cheeks, Samson started licking my face as if to comfort me. "That's my good Samson boy."

Delilah sat calmly, looking around as though she were keeping an eye out for intruders, anyone who might hurt us. "That's my good Little Dee." I couldn't have been more proud or happier with my two loves on that day.

Chapter 10
The Co-op Board

People leave imprints on our lives, shaping who we become in much the same way that a symbol is pressed into the page of a book to tell you who it comes from.

Dogs, however, leave paw prints on our lives and our souls, which are as unique as fingerprints in every way.

Ashley Lorezana, Author

Two weeks after my first letter from the Co-op Board, I received another complaint letter telling me that something had to be done about the dogs' barking. I decided to go to the next Board meeting to meet them face-to-face. I was sitting in the back of the room when the issue of Samson and Delilah's barking came up.

The attorney for the Board said he had heard from me. He was complimentary about my letter and stated that I was doing a lot to rectify the situation. I raised my hand and explained that they were not barking as much.

A neighbor who I recognized quickly spoke up, "She's right. It's not her dogs. It's a dog in the building behind ours. The sound of barking comes in through the windows. After all, it's summer."

That was that. I never heard from the Board again. It was New York, but it had been that easy.

Walks in the park and play dates with other dogs were definitely helping us keep Samson from racing around our apartment. After a long walk, we found him snuggled down in a favorite spot, his paws going and his nose twitching, happily and deeply immersed in one of his dreams.

Not only did we walk them at least twice a day for at least a half-hour, but on Saturday and Sunday mornings, we took them to an area in Central Park near 72d Street where dogs were allowed off the lead before 9 a.m. There Samson met with many other dogs.

His main objective was to get one or more of them to chase him. He ran at lightning speed and, no matter how large, rarely could any other dog catch him.

While Samson was busy running and playing, Delilah stayed on the sidelines, sniffing around the trees and chasing squirrels, content to be nearby and on her own. We stood around watching the dogs enjoying their time together and talking with their human companions.

Seldom did we see the same people and dogs, but then, it was New York and Central Park. There were millions of people residing in the tall apartment buildings running from 59th Street to 104th Street on both the East and West Sides.

One weekday morning I took the dogs on my own to a spot near the reservoir in the park. Guess what? Samson lifted his leg. I applauded him and chuckled. After all, he was a boy.

Farther on, a number of dogs were running and playing off the lead. It was before nine o'clock. Samson immediately joined in the fun, and then suddenly, he started howling.

All the dogs came running to him, except Delilah, of course. The dog owners started to laugh, and several were saying, "What's happening?"

I chuckled, "He's calling the pack. Beagles howl to call other dogs to join them."
Delilah did not join him because he was not in charge of her—in fact, she was their pack leader, and she had not said a word.

One October day, all four of us were returning from a walk to the carousel. Everywhere we looked, there were mounds of leaves—gold, russet, and red. As usual, Samson was sniffing around a tree, his nose buried in the leaves.

All of a sudden, we heard him yelp. Then we saw something flying in the air near him. We raced over and saw blood streaming from his nose and a rat on the ground with two teeth marks on its side.

I shouted, "Let's get him home and call the vet?"

"How do we stop the bleeding?" cried David.

I noticed that Samson kept licking his nose. "I think he'll take care of the blood, and it won't need stitches. I'm concerned about rabies? Don't rats have rabies?" I yelled out as we raced along the path.

"Well, he's had his rabies shot?"

"Isn't there still a problem?"

We were definitely naive about rats and rabies. As we hurried back, we talked about what must have happened and decided that the rat had been buried in the leaves, probably eating something, maybe even asleep. Samson got a whiff of the food or the rat, and when he went to check it out, the rat bit him. Startled, he bit the rat and tossed it up in the air.

We were about twelve blocks from home. I checked his nose every few minutes and the bleeding stopped a few blocks from our apartment. It took us about fifteen minutes before we got home, and immediately David called the vet. He explained that rats in New York City usually do not have rabies, and there was no need to worry. We had another Samson story to tell our friends.

Years ago, when I first moved to New York, a friend told me there were a million stories in New York, and I was trying to have all of them. This comment was prompted by the many situations I found myself in as a new New Yorker. The same could be said of Samson and Delilah.

Chapter 11
Time Wasters

Money can buy you a fine dog, but only love can make him wag his tail.
Kinky Friedman

Day after day, David and I stopped what we were doing and petted and hugged the dogs. Often David chuckled and said to me, "They're time-wasters."

"But what a way to waste time," I retorted, and we hugged them to us. That time with them was so special. The more time we spent with them, the more we wanted to spend.

We lived on the top floor of a six-story Tudor building. There were two elevators on each floor, one at each end of the long hallway. We discovered that one of the challenges of living there with dogs was the elevator.

One of the two elevators was just outside our door, so getting the dogs into the elevator should not have been a problem. Wishful thinking! Our immediate problem became the other dogs already living in the building and also riding the elevator.

The first few months, we had not noticed any problem. Then suddenly, without warning, Delilah started sniffing at the elevator door. She started barking incessantly—her little body gyrating when she smelled a dog.

Samson began to howl. He was howling, I'm sure, because he wanted to play with a dog, any dog or meet and greet a human. On the other hand, Delilah was signaling that demons were lurking somewhere.

We attempted to solve that problem by David going out of the apartment door first and calling the elevator. At the same time, I waited inside with the dogs. When the elevator arrived and was empty, David would call out to me. That worked okay most of the time, but if Delilah got a whiff of a dog anywhere in the building, she would start barking.

Sometimes when in the elevator it would stop on the way down, and another dog would be on the other side of the door. Then she would bark and lunge at the door, pulling on the lead. She had no fear, no matter how large or snarky the other dog might be.

"She's afraid. That's why she barks," I remarked to David.

"How can we get rid of her fear?"

"Well, that's a tough one." I knew she felt trapped inside the elevator, and indeed she was. There was only one way out, which involved walking by the dog she was afraid of. We needed to keep her out of that situation at the elevator. We needed to redirect her attention, but that was difficult to do because she was so afraid.

Over the next few weeks, we decided when she started barking, we would take the stairs instead of using the elevator, at least for a few floors. At other times, we walked to the elevator at the other end of the building, hoping there would be no dog there, nor even the scent of one. As always, we were concerned about complaints about the dogs.

The minute Delilah smelled another dog, or I saw one in the hallway or outside the building, I asked her to sit. I chuckled as I watched her screw her bottom in the dirt or pavement, trying so hard to do what I was asking of her. I then gave her a favorite treat, just little bits, repeatedly to keep her attention.

At other times, I would turn and walk in the opposite direction, trying to divert her attention. Sometimes that worked, and at other times she would continue to bark and ignore me, and only she knew why.

We soon discovered that one of the dogs that caused Delilah to bark incessantly was a huge German Shepherd that had moved into the building. He was at least three feet long and over three feet high—one of the most giant dogs I had ever seen. I, too, found him a bit frightening on the other side of the elevator door.

When Delilah barked and lunged at him, his owner just smiled. It was a bit comic, little Delilah taking on that big German Shepherd. A few weeks earlier, I had met the wife of the owner plus the dog that lived with the German Shepherd. It was a Lhasa Apso. That little dog did the same thing as Delilah, so he understood.

One day we saw the Shepherd and his human companion just inside the park entrance, so I decided to try redirecting Delilah's behavior again. I used a treat to get her to sit again and again. Every time she got up, I offered the treat and asked her to sit.

After a few tries, I decided to walk her over to meet the big dog. I thought she wouldn't feel as confined in the park as she did in the elevator. Maybe that would make a difference.

Delilah greeted the Shepherd quietly, and her tail started to wag. That lasted about a minute, and then she couldn't help herself. She started barking. Why I'll never know. The Shepherd's owner and I both laughed and went our separate ways, but I was delighted Delilah had made some progress.

Chapter 12

First Christmas

> *I have found that when you are deeply troubled, there are things you get from the silent devoted companionship of a dog that you can get from no other source."*
> Doris Day

One day, I noticed that Delilah had her tongue way down into Samson's ear and was cleaning out the wax. Like my first two dogs, they cleaned each other's ears because I had never found any icky stuff inside.

When I started lifting up Samson's ear and saying to Delilah, "Pooey, pooey," she would race over and clean out his ears. He did the same for her without asking.

Our first Christmas together, and our first with the dogs, we had bought stockings for all of us. Samson's was red, green, and white checks with paws printed on the squares. Delilah's stocking was in the shape of an elf shoe, burgundy trimmed in green velvet. Our stockings were deep red with patchwork Santa's—David's being larger than mine so I could fit big candy bars in his.

We visited with my mother and family over Christmas but returned for New Year's Eve. We decided to make a reservation at a favorite restaurant that I had introduced David to near Times Square.

Around ten o'clock, we had finished dinner and were ready to leave but the owners of the restaurant tried to convince us to stay until midnight. Although it was festive, we looked at each other.

"Just the check," David said as he grabbed my hand. "Let's go home and see the dogs."

Once home, we made a fire in the fireplace and welcomed in the New Year, snuggling down with our two loves.

David and I enjoy giving dinner parties at least once a month for friends and new acquaintances.

We allowed the dogs on the loveseat when it was just the four of us. Then when visitors arrived, I made an effort to keep the dogs on their beds because some people don't want a dog in their face.

Delilah immediately climbed on the lap of any person she had determined was willing to have her or who could with a little encouragement. I requested that she get down, but within a few seconds, she had won the heart of a guest.

Secretly, we knew that she was welcoming that person into the pack. I thought it best not to share that tidbit. Instead, I let the guest believe Delilah was enamored with their presence. After all, adoration makes us all feel better, but Delilah was the one being adored.

Our guest, bewitched by her sweetness—she knew how to pick them—had become her lifetime friend. I offered to take Delilah and put her on her bed and then I would hear comments such as, *"Oh, I don't mind. She can stay." "She's fine here, really."*

Samson would respond by jumping on the couch immediately, trying to nudge Delilah out of the way, as if to say, *"me too, me too."*

Earlier, we had given Samson the nickname, "Me too!" He always wanted what Delilah had, whether it was pets, treats, a cuddle, or a lap to sit on.

"Um!" I said to David later. "Does Delilah know the difference between the lap and the couch? Can she understand why she's allowed on the couch now and not later? Can Samson understand why Delilah and not him? I don't think so!"

They were just like children. Even if there was an explanation, and we could explain it to them, would it matter? Yes, we were being inconsistent. We were all complicit in playing favorites by allowing Delilah and not Samson. In his own way, Samson knew

Chapter 13

Championing Delilah

The one absolutely unselfish friend that man can have in this selfish world, the one that never deserts him, the one that never proves ungrateful or treacherous ... is his dog...

He will kiss the hand that has no food to offer...

He guards the sleep of his pauper master as if he were a prince. When all other friends desert, he remains....

Senator George Graham Vest, Missouri

Early one new year, we had some friends over for a dinner party. Most everyone enjoyed meeting and greeting the dogs, and we always gave each guest a goodie to give to the dogs as a way of introduction. It also got them to sit and settle down—both!

Two of the guests—a couple I had met the previous June—arrived with a lemon meringue pie that immediately interested Samson. The wife, Carolyn, was besotted with Samson's good looks and playfulness.

Every time I glanced in her direction, Carolyn was rubbing Samson under his chin and cooing into his ear. He had made his way onto the couch beside her, and he stayed by her side before and after dinner, being adored.

James, her husband, was not at all taken by the dogs, so as with non-doggie guests, we did our best to keep

Samson away. Delilah was quick to wiggle her bottom if anyone came near. Although comfortable greeting guests with enthusiasm and pushing her way next to them, she quickly knew when she wasn't wanted. She would take her cue and walk away and find a place to snuggle down in the den.

A few weeks after the dinner party, the four of us got together to play bridge. David is an avid bridge player and was interested in playing again, and the three of us wanted to learn. They come over around 4 o'clock to take a walk in the park and spend time playing bridge.

Carolyn walked through the door and hugged Samson to her. She gave him all the attention he desires, but she ignored Delilah. Finally, I said to her, "You know, I have two dogs."

It just came out, but I knew deep down that I am a champion for inclusivity and the underdog (pun intended). The person or dog or child who is not in the spotlight, the one who doesn't get the attention, is the one I champion, and Delilah was just that kind of dog. She wasn't as pretty as Samson was handsome, and she was quiet and demure, unlike Samson's... let's say pushiness, for lack of a better word.

James, her husband, didn't fuss over or pet either dog. For months after, Samson tried his darndest to change that. On the couch, he edged closer and closer every visit, but James continued to resist Samson's overtures of friendship.

One evening after playing bridge for a few hours, we sat and talked, the dogs gathered around. The second

James had sat down, Samson jumped up and planted himself right next to him, abandoning Carolyn.

The three of us watched this happening again and again. Finally, on that one particular evening, James reached over and petted Samson's ear. The three of us burst out laughing. Samson had finally won him over.

The more we were with Samson and Delilah, the more enjoyable the day, so we rarely left the apartment without them. If we went grocery shopping, they came along. David stayed outside or walked them up and down the street.

Most often, people stopped and talked and petted the dogs. They definitely knew how to draw strangers to them and us.

It was a beautiful sunny day in July, and we were at the street fair that goes from 86th Street to 72nd along Broadway. David was checking out an item while I stood to the side, holding the dogs' leads and looking at the passersby. An elderly woman came up to me, somewhat out of breath, and said, "How much do you want for your dogs?"

"Pardon me," I started to chuckle and then decided she was not joking. "You're serious? You really want to buy our dogs."

"Yes, I've been watching you walk them down the street for the last several blocks, and they are such gorgeous and well-behaved dogs."

"I'm sorry. We would never want to sell our dogs. There's not enough money in the world to tempt us."

She smiled, "I didn't think you would, but it was worth a chance. What I wouldn't give for two dogs like yours. I'm too old to train them. It would be great to get them perfect."

"Well, thank you," I chuckled, "but they're not perfect, but then neither are we."

She gave them one last pet, and we said our goodbyes. I turned around to find David behind me. "What did that lady want?"

"Our dogs."

I told him the story, and I believe we walked a few feet higher in the air, knowing someone saw what we always believed. They were great dogs.

Chapter 14

Cueing and Cluing

Dogs are not our whole life, but they make our lives whole.
Roger Caras, Animal Advocate

During our walks, I noticed that Samson was afraid of everyone who wore a large hat with a brim. He cowered and sometimes even growled just under his breath. No bearing of teeth, but it was obvious he was afraid.

I mentioned this to David, and we started to wonder if someone wearing a hat had beaten him or harmed him in some way. We had no way of knowing; we just had to note the possibility.

Often, we took the dogs to a street fair if nearby. On one particular day, we decided to let them stay in the air-conditioned apartment.

Outside, the temperature was in the 90s. Although we had heard only mad dogs and Englishmen (David being English) go out in the noonday sun, we knew not to take our loves out on the hot New York pavement.

During the outing, I bought two big floppy hats. One I decided to wear rather than carry it. We arrived back home around 5:30 p.m. The sun was going down and was coming through the ten-by-ten window, casting me in shadow.

Samson came running, hearing the door open. When he saw me, he stopped and started to bark and then growl. I called out, "Samson boy. It's me." He stopped and then started to bark again.

Then David yelled, "It's OK, Samson."

Only when he was close enough to smell us did he stop.

I took off my hat, and David and I got on our knees, petting him and cooing in his ears, "Good Samson boy."

"What was that all about?" David said.

"The hat, I think. I've seen it again and again how Samson cowers or moves away from someone with a hat."

"But why bark at you?"

I looked around the room. "Well, it's somewhat dark. I must have appeared in silhouette. I looked like a big black blob. Then there's the hat. It morphed my head into a figure he didn't recognize."

"But it's still you."

"Yes, but he couldn't tell the difference until he heard our voices and then smelled us. I've been told dogs only see in black and white, shades of gray — no color. That guy on the street with the grocery cart is black and wears a big hat and dark colors.

"Samson only sees a huge dark image with a hat, so that's why he always cowers. I noticed the same reaction when a man has a hood over his head. He cringes as we walk by."

I remember that dogs don't see as far or as clearly as we do. There's a layer over their eyes to protect them from getting scratched by a twig or bush. Their sense of smell, especially beagles, is their strongest sense, then hearing, and then sight. I also read a book a while back which mentioned that the figure of a person with a hood often scares a dog."

"So, how can we make him unafraid?"

"I don't think that will ever be possible. We cannot reason with Samson. He only trusts his senses and his sight—what he sees. It's what he reacts to first. Smell only cued him that it was us because we got close enough."

"So, there's nothing we can do?"

"Try to limit those encounters," but, of course, we couldn't.

A month later, we agreed to host an organization's dinner meeting at our apartment for over thirty people. Food from several restaurants was ordered, and I hired someone to help out. The apartment had wall-to-wall people. They were talking and eating and generally enjoying each other's company, except for one.

As I came out of the kitchen, I saw a man with the blackest of black toupees standing about four inches off the top of his head and puffing out at the sides. He was reading the titles of all the books on the shelves in the hallway. Next to him was Samson, fixated on his every move.

The guest looked up as I walked by. "Do you know you have a first edition?"

While speaking, I noticed that Samson's eyes were still glued on him, and then I heard a soft growl. I had not experienced this with Samson when guests were in the apartment. He usually wanted to lick them to death. As I looked at the man's toupee—finding it difficult not to—I realize that it probably resembled a hat to Samson.

I ushered Samson into the bedroom, where he remained, although guests who were smitten with him kept going in and visiting. No problems with any of them, but I could not help thinking our lovely boy was being frightened again and again.

Samson was growling out of fear. We could not reason with him, so we could not remove his fear. All we could try to do was to limit those times, if and when we could, or move him out of that situation as quickly as possible.

Both Samson and Delilah rolled on their backs or wagged their tails when I said with a lilt of playfulness in my voice, "You're the best doggies." When Samson came running to me with a toy or was running with other dogs, he was totally immersed in those endeavors.

Samson and Delilah were continually *cueing* or *cluing* us as to what motivated them—what they responded to. We needed to pay attention to what they were saying and were not saying. We needed to observe their behavior and determine what excited them and moved them toward action. It took effort and time, but in the end, it was worth it. They were worth it.

When I came home, they raced to me to get first dibs on pets. Samson often jumped over Delilah if he didn't get there first. "Me too, me too," he was saying. When I petted both of them, there was no need to compete or wait.

We had a love-fest filled with laughter and cuddles and pets. It bonded them to me, and I believe they felt safe in my arms.

Chapter 15

Training the Master

I don't believe in the concept of hell, but if I did, I would think of it as filled with people who were cruel to animals.
Immanuel Kant

When I said to Delilah, "Let's go snuggle, buggle," it was impossible to stop her from running and cuddling next to me.

When I asked Samson to get a toy, he raced around to find one. When I stepped on their paws, I said, "Sorry, sorry, sorry," and they came running for a hug. When Samson nipped me in play, I would say "sorry, sorry, sorry," and he would lick my hand.

Such happiness!

Once when David returned from one of his business trips, I announced to him, "I realize that you're right. I'm the center of their world because I spend more time with them."

David was the director of management training for a large corporation and had to go to the office every day when he was not traveling. I was a management consultant and executive coach with my own business.

When not on the road, I was in my home office writing my workshop materials, coaching by phone, and doing whatever needed to be done. Not only was I ever-present in Samson and Delilah's lives, I decided when and how much they went out and what they ate and did the majority of the time.

I went on to say to David, "I think they also need to see you as their master too. Right now, you just walk them in the morning when you are here. I feed them and do most of the training. They see me as their master but not you."

"So, what do you want me to do?"

"Why don't you give them treats after dinner? If they see you as a source of food, they will come to see you as their master as well. Right now, it's me they follow around and listen to. You also need to do some training and reinforce my training."

The ritual of the treats gave birth the next day. Initially, David called them to him, made them sit, said their names, and gave each a treat. A few weeks later, while David was clearing the dishes and cleaning the kitchen after dinner, Delilah came to him and danced around. Ignoring her did not deter her efforts. At this point, David was not sure what she wanted.

"Do you want to go out?" he asked her and went to the door. Delilah did not follow.

"What do you want?" he asked again, looking down at her.

She let out a soft bark. Her bottom wiggled, and she wouldn't stop until David gave them the treats. It was then that David gave her the name *"the nagger."*

Dogs are creatures of habit. They respond to structure—the same thing every day, at the same time, so the treat had become a habit she wasn't about to give up. Laughingly, I realized that rituals were important to dogs too. The same thing day in, day out makes them feel secure—something they can count on.

Delilah was adorable as she did her begging *dance*, but it also triggered in me another thought. I chuckled, "David, you are now trained. She has trained you to give them the evening treats."

"But I would give them every day anyway."

"Yes, I know. I love seeing the dogs sitting there—all eyes fixed on you."

One day while coaxing Delilah to eat, I gave her another name, "fussy britches." She was a finicky eater. I know the very idea of a beagle being a finicky eater seems silly—but yes, she was. She smelled the treat or food first, took a bite, looked up or around, ate some more, sometimes took a drink, and so on.

Samson had no such hesitation. He ate everything in his bowl within seconds and always finished first. He then nudged his way towards Delilah's bowl. It only took a few corrections from us and a bark from Delilah to get Samson to stay out of her bowl. All we had to say to him was, *"Respect the bowl, Samson."*

I was delighted they were learning so quickly. Besides hugs and pets, we used treats to teach them, and they were everywhere—in commercials, on the shelves, friends brought them. Treats no doubt got Samson and Delilah's attention, but to what end?

During a grocery outing, we were looking at dog treats. David picked up a package and brought it over.

"Do you think Delilah would like this one?"

I felt the bag, trying to determine the size of the treats inside, and then I read the label. "I know we love shopping for the dogs, especially finding something Delilah likes, but....."

"Should we give them treats?"

"It's more about how much, how often, and for what? Most treats have so much grain in them and other stuff I can't identify. I don't want them to get fat."

"But we walk them miles every day, and it has improved their behavior."

"Well, the treats do get their attention, but after a while, I want them to do what we ask just because."

"There's that consulting hat again."

I smiled. "Well, yes, of course. If we always use food to get the dogs to do what we want, soon we'll have a dog that will only perform for food and an overweight, unhealthy dog. That's no different from employees who perform just for money."

"So, should I put back all these?" David said as I looked down at the five bags of treats in the cart.

"No, I'm just saying let's use them at times to get their attention or teach them something new but not all the time. We'll use pets and hugs and praise more often. I know you'll never want to stop gathering them around you after dinner. That is fine."

A few days later, I called David at the office. "I've decided to write a book. *All I ever needed to know about management I learned from my dogs.*"

"I think that's a great idea!"

"I was joking, although I must admit the similarities are many. Every day they crystallize for me so many of the ideas I've been espousing for years about management."

"Then write it."

Chapter 16

Let is Snow!

"The greatest fear dogs know is the fear that you will not come back when you go out the door without them."
                    Stanley Coren

The months were passing quickly, and David was traveling more often. Fortunately, I was traveling less.

It was evident that when we packed a suitcase, Delilah paced and seemed agitated. She came to us, wiggled her bottom, and sniffed the suitcase. Other times she was calm or settled on her bed or a favorite spot.

We finally decided that when she saw a suitcase, she knew one of us was leaving her. We decided to pack out of her sight and hide the suitcase in the closet.

When David was ready to leave, I played with the dogs while he sneaked the suitcase into the hallway. What else could we do for someone we love so?

Winter in New York City has its challenges, and it became evident that on the cold and dark and damp streets, the dogs needed coats. The wind whips around, especially when you turn the corner, and the chill seems to invade the bones of both dogs and humans. We went to a pet store trying to find doggie coats.

David was always ready to buy. "Let's take this one."

"But it's not cute enough. It's not warm enough. It looks too big, too small," whatever, I could not settle on a coat. Finally, I decided to order the coats from an online pet store.

Delilah's was a beautiful shade of red, lined with deep blue soft material. When I put it on her, she pranced around, and we decided that Delilah indeed loved to dress up.

Samson's coat was black, lined with soft red material, and, he reminded me of Dracula in his cloak. He looked at me as if to say, "This coat is for sissies," but he looked so handsome, and as it was snowy, we insisted. Their coats also kept their bellies from getting mucked up with ice, snow, and cinders as they walked along the streets.

The coats solved only one of the winter problems. Walking the dogs on the streets presented another challenge in the snow. The sidewalks are salted, and salt burns the dogs' paws. Also, when they came in, they would lick their wet paws, ingesting the salt, which had chemicals in it, so we had to wash off all eight paws.

That first winter with them, there was a lot of snow—more than New York City had seen in decades. One day we were walking in the park, and they were racing around in over a foot of snow. Delilah, who was short to the ground, was hopping like a bunny to make her way through the deep drifts.

All of a sudden, she squealed out. As I raced to her, she collapsed and continued to squeal. Within seconds Samson started to yelp as well, and David raced to him.

We discovered that the fur between their pads had collected snow that turned to ice as they played in the cold. That ice was burning them and causing them pain. I pull off my one glove and reached for Delilah's paw.

"Try to melt the ice and snow with the warmth of your hand."

"It's working," shouted David, about ten feet away. "Let's get them back to the apartment."

I picked up Delilah in my arms. David picked up Samson, and we walked as quickly as we could back to the apartment.

"The squealing sound makes my heartache," I shouted to David. "Our little doggies in such pain…."

A few days later, I was walking them by myself, and within seconds both dogs cried out at the same time. Which dog to help first? An older woman walking in the park heard their squeals. She scurried up to me, asking what was happening. I explained, and she took hold of both leads, so I could use both hands to warm their paws.

We had to find booties for them to wear. We tried several pairs at a local pet shop, but none would stay on. Once again, I ordered them online, and they arrived in two days. So, we had to figure out how to get eight little booties on their paws.

David held one of the dogs on his lap while I put on one bootie at a time. They went on easy enough. Adjusting the Velcro strap, so they would stay on was the biggest challenge. Often the first one would fall off before I could get the second one on.

Neither dog resisted our efforts, but once they were all on and we released Delilah, she put on quite a show. She lifted up one paw at a time, then another, then another and would do this for at least a minute.

I'm sure if she could have lifted all four paws at one time, she would have. In her own gentle way, I suppose she was reacting to something strange on her paws. Samson never bothered about the booties.

Our next challenge was the deep snow. Often Samson and Delilah chased squirrels into the snowbanks. Sometimes they would return with one or more booties missing. One of us would then have to search to find them, often digging down deep with snow beyond our wrists.

It was tiresome, but they loved the snow, especially Delilah, who raced around in circles. Each would put their nose deep into the snow, trying to pick up a scent. We delighted in their fun, but we were always mindful that they might squeal out having lost a bootie and having a frozen paw.

One day we were walking north towards the pond when Samson spied some ducks. The edge of the pond was starting to freeze and was covered with snow. He ran towards the ducks, and before we knew it, he had sunk into the water — the thin ice having given away under his weight. You should have seen his face. Shock is the only word to describe him. We quickly pulled him out and raced home to get him dry. We had another Samson Boy story.

Chapter 17
The Doorman or a Visitor

"If you think dogs can't count, try putting three dog biscuits in your pocket and then give him only two of them."
Phil Pastoret, Illustrator

After a few months, we discovered that Samson had taught himself that when the phone rang twice, someone would soon appear at our door. Of course, he did not know that when the phone rang twice, it was our doorman telling us a guest was coming, but indeed he knew that someone would soon arrive. We knew he understood because when the phone rang normally, with only one ring, he ignored it and did not go to the door. How clever our Samson Boy was!

One day I was walking Samson and Delilah by myself. The two immediately started to chase after a squirrel. An older woman without a dog came towards me. "Don't let your dogs chase squirrels. They're vicious."

I nodded, "Yes, I've heard that."

She continued, "One day, I was walking my dog, and a squirrel attacked her. She was ripped apart by that squirrel. I could not get her away. She had over thirty stitches."

"Oh my, how awful! We try to be careful."

We had heard squirrels can be vicious and do not back down. There were times when a squirrel started coming back down the tree, looking ready to do battle. We pulled the dogs away quickly and went on in the opposite direction."

I thanked her for cautioning me and after each getting a pet, we said goodbye.

On our dog outings, people were constantly stopping us, petting the dogs, admiring them for their calmness and gentle demeanor. Others wanted to know what type of dog Samson was because he was so gorgeous.

When one of us said, "Beagle," we usually saw a puzzled look. So, we explained that although he did not resemble the stocky, low-to-the-ground English beagle that most people knew, he was a beagle. He could have been a show dog, but then we would never have done that to our sweet boy.

We wished we had a nickel for the many times we heard someone say, "I had a beagle when I was little." At one time, especially in the '50s, beagles reigned for several years as the number one dog. I guess the popularity of Snoopy created that phenomenon.

Then, beagles fell out of favor to dogs considered cuter, smaller, larger, prettier, unique…. I said to David, "I want to write a book, 'Bring Back the Beagle.' They are such wonderful dogs."

During our second summer with Samson and Delilah, full-size, painted plastic cows had appeared throughout New York City—many in Central Park and some on the street. We were always delighted when we walked along a street or turned a corner and there before us was a painted cow—some in bright colors and all with scenes and a theme.

Besides the street fairs and walks in the park, we enjoyed going to the theater, and, of course, we were always keen to get half-priced tickets. One day I took the subway down to TKTS—the half-price ticket booth in midtown, while David was walking Samson and Delilah the fifty blocks through the park to meet me.

He turned the corner at 72nd Street and in front of them was one of those painted cows. Samson started howling and would not stop. He got closer to the cow and tried to get a whiff. Then he backed away—all the time howling.

As David told me the story, he could not stop laughing. "I'm sure some people thought Samson was being killed or hurt because his howl was so piercing. A crowd gathered around us, everybody amused by Samson's antics." Our poor little, frightened boy—what must he have been experiencing?

That summer, I decided to attend a writing workshop in Glastonbury, England. I would be gone for ten days, and David would be in charge. I was not concerned about that because all our time and effort had rewarded us now with two easy dogs, so I was surprised at the news when I called home one day.

"So, how are the dogs?" I asked—my usual first question.

"They're fine, but you won't believe what Delilah did. She chewed the spine off my Ogden Nash book. It's about forty years old. It can't be replaced."

"Can it be repaired? Can you tape the spine?"

"Not really. The pages are also ripped. Remember the poem I left on your answering machine when we first got together?"

"Of course, I remember. How could I forget it?"

"Well, it's been shredded."

David was so upset. I know his old books, like mine, have special meanings.

"What's the name of the book?"

"The Works of Ogden Nash."

After we hung up, I headed to the used bookstore in Glastonbury. I had been there twice before, but this time I was on a mission.

After spending about a half-hour without finding what I was looking for, I walked down the steps and spoke to the clerk.

"I'm looking for anything that has the poems of Ogden Nash."

"We get books all the time, so keep checking."

I smile, "I'm just here for another five days. My dog chewed the spine off one of my husband's favorite Ogden Nash books. He's English and bought it in England many years ago, so I want to surprise him with a replacement."

"I guess your dog likes horse glue."

Confused by what I heard, I said, "What do you mean, horse glue?"

"Well, the glue used was probably made from old horses, especially years ago, so that's why she chewed the spine."

I chuckled, "So, she wasn't being a bad dog. She was just hungry."

That's when we decided that we needed to move the books from the bottom shelves of the bookcases to where Delilah couldn't get at them. Funny of all the things Samson chewed, it was never a book. I guess Delilah's halo was a little tilted.

Chapter 18
David and I Say "I Do"

One reason a dog can be such a comfort when you're feeling blue is that he doesn't try to find out why.
Unknown

In the fall of that same year, David and I decided we would get married on New Year's Eve. It was to be a small affair—just close family—some from England—and one of my long-time friends and her husband.

Because of the difficulties of moving even just our twenty guests around New York City on New Year's Eve, we decided to have the ceremony and the dinner afterward catered in our apartment. Of course, the most heartwarming outcome of that decision was that Samson and Delilah could attend.

David's daughter, and his son-in-law, plus his grandchildren—a girl and two boys—were staying with us. It was a full house indeed, and one of our challenges was to get Lucy, the youngest grandchild, to fall asleep the first night of their visit.

Delilah helped out there. We put her in bed with Lucy, and when Lucy was asleep, we removed Delilah and put her in bed next to one of the two boys, Julian or Tiffer, while Samson snuggled down with the other.

My relatives were staying at a hotel a few blocks away that did not allow dogs, so Annie, my nephew's dog, came two days later and loved playing with Samson. He had finally met his match for energy, and the two of them romped and played and kept the children entertained.

The night before the wedding, we took all our guests to dinner and then to the Christmas program with the Rockettes at Radio City. When we arrived back at the apartment, I found a puddle of blood in the bathroom about the size of a saucer. I panicked and cried out, "One of the dogs is very ill. There's blood everywhere."

Which dog we did not know. My nephew and his wife quickly took the dogs outside and discovered that it was Delilah who had been passing blood. I called the emergency vet number. They told me that even if we brought her in and ran tests, they might not know why this was happening. "Feed her some boiled chicken and rice" was the suggestion.

That was a long night, worrying about her, so the next day, we decided to take her to our vet because there was still blood. Again, finding a taxi in New York that would pick us up with a dog is a challenge. So, while I stood hidden with Delilah under my coat, David flagged down the taxi, and then I ran to it with Delilah in my arms. "Let him throw us out," I said to David.

The vet, concerned that Delilah was dehydrated, put liquid into her and recommended some canned dog food—chicken with rice—some bland food. We wondered if it might have been the children and the arrival of another dog and the excitement of the evening that unsettled Delilah. Like me, she liked a quiet life.

The vet said, "That could be it. It also could be that she ate something too rich. With kids around, maybe they slipped her too much people-food."

After arriving back at the apartment, we asked the children's parents to take them out for the day, so Delilah could rest. My nephew and his wife took Samson and Annie for a long walk, minimizing the racing around. Later that day, Delilah had some more chicken and rice, and we could tell she was feeling better, although there was still some blood.

Since that event, bland chicken and rice has been our go-to treatment whenever any dog is ill.

On the evening of the wedding, the candles were lit throughout our apartment. We had spoken to the minister at length about the ceremony, sharing with her our quirky beginning and what to her was our apparent differences and individuality. It was a lovely, intimate affair.

David read the Ogden Nash poem he had left on my answering machine several years earlier, which ended with a marriage proposal. Another poem—that I had left on David's machine explaining my position on marriage—was also read. Those in attendance could not help but laugh, knowing both of us so well. It was the most special memory of that day.

My favorite picture of our wedding was with Samson on my lap and Delilah on David's.

Chapter 19
Yes, it's a Racoon!

Dogs possess a quality that's rare among humans—the ability to make you feel valued just by being you—and it was something of a miracle to me to be on the receiving end of all that acceptance. The dog didn't care what I looked like, or what a train wreck of a life I'd led before I got her, or what we did from day-to-day. She just wanted to be with me, and that awareness gave me a singular sensation of delight.
　　　　　　　　　Caroline Knapp

One of my greatest joys, although there are many, was snuggling with Samson and Delilah in the still of the morning. Delilah would tuck into the curve of my chest and belly, and Samson came close to my face as I petted and cooed their names and whispered, "Good doggies, good doggies. You're the best doggies."

Scaffolding had been put up on our side of the building during the summer so the brick could be repointed. David was away on a business trip, and the dogs were snuggled in bed with me. Sometime after 5 a.m. I was awakened by a non-identifiable scratching sound.

I felt around the bed. Samson and Delilah were still there. Delilah was snoring, and Samson was also in a deep sleep. After listening for about thirty seconds, I decided that someone, something was scratching at the living room window. My two loves were still fast asleep, so I crept out of bed and went to the window.

Outside in the metal flower box, I could see a black blob that looked something like an armadillo's back. Then it hit me—it was a raccoon.

I had heard from one of the doormen that a raccoon had come through a neighbor's window a few days before. I also knew from talking to Animal Control people in the park one day, they had to remove rabid racoons that had come out in the day.

The raccoon was scratching so hard I was afraid it might break through the side panels of the air conditioner and get inside. In the dark, I couldn't see what damage it had already done.

I didn't want the raccoon and the dogs meeting should it get in. I knew that raccoons, like squirrels, could rip a dog apart. I also knew they could be rabid. Unlike the dogs, I had not had my shots.

"What to do?" I pounded on the window above, trying to scare the raccoon away. It did not move. I was also concerned that it might get into another neighbor's apartment open window.

I decided to call the CACC—Center for Animal Care and Control, where we had adopted Samson and Delilah. A recorded message stated that due to the mayor's cuts in funding, they could not respond and instead recommended calling 911.

"Call 911" I said to myself. "This is not that kind of emergency," but I had no choice as the scratching continued.

Fortunately, the dogs were still asleep. That's what a three-hour walk in the park can do for dogs! Better than any tranquilizer or sleeping pill!

I could not get through the first time I dialed 911—so I tried a second time. Still, I could not speak with anyone. I called our doorman. "What do you want me to do?" definitely agitated. I had disturbed his sleep.

"So, it's not your job to get rid of raccoons."

He didn't answer.

"Maybe, you could make sure the superintendent and workers who are going to go up that scaffolding this morning know about this." Again, no response, so I hung up.

A few minutes later, the phone rang. Samson and Delilah stirred. "I've got some police down here who want to come up."

As I hung up, I realized the doorman who just called was a different doorman from the one I had spoken to about five minutes earlier. It was just after 6 a.m., and the shift had changed.

I sequestered the dogs in the bedroom. To stop the police from ringing the doorbell and the dogs from barking, I went to the door and opened it. What a sight. I was smiling, chuckling inside.

Four policemen—New York City's finest—were coming down the hall, and they were packing—guns and

Billy clubs. Beside them was the doorman—at least a foot shorter than the policemen.

I thought four policemen was a little over-the-top for a raccoon, but there they were. They came in, and I directed them towards the window. One of them walked over and looked. "Yeah, that's a raccoon, alright."

"So, what can you do?"

"Nothing really!"

"But the CACC's message said that you guys take care of these matters."

"Not us," and they turned and walked out the door.

As the sun came up, the raccoon started its way across the scaffolding and disappeared. The sun had done what New York's finest could not.

On our walks in Central Park, I took bags with me so we could bring home pinecones and chestnuts of all sizes. After a few weeks, I had quite a collection. I decided to use them for a thanksgiving arrangement along the big maple counter between the kitchen and the dining room. It was visible from both rooms.

Once I started to arrange the display, I saw Delilah standing on her back legs, her nose twitching and her ears perked up. Samson joined her, their tails wagging and their noses wiggling non-stop as they eyed the pinecones and chestnuts.

"David, look at the dogs."

"What do you think they smell?"

I started to laugh. "Squirrels, raccoons, whatever was up in those trees in the park."

The remaining three years in New York were much of the same. My mother passed away, bringing sadness into my life. I remember her visit and how the two dogs sat beside her on the love seat as she crocheted.

David was still traveling quite a bit, and we finally decided that it was time for him to retire. He didn't want to stay in New York City, so we started looking for property in New England. Samson and Delilah traveled with us every time we searched for a new home.

We finally found a historic home with a small yard in a mid-size New England town. I miss New York in some ways, especially Central Park and the many hours we spent with the dogs. In our new home, we would have a fenced garden. Samson and Delilah would be free of the lead more often than not.

You may remember that we did not pack suitcases in front of Delilah, but one evening in our rush to get packed to move, we forgot. We brought the suitcases out of the closet and started packing them with clothes from the chest of drawers and dresser.

When I turned around to put more clothes in one of the suitcases, I found Delilah curled in a ball and snuggled down in the clothes inside the suitcase. Insurmountable love for her welled up in my heart. Then I started to chuckle through my tears.

"Look, David! I guess if we're going somewhere, she's going to make sure she goes with us."

We both got down on our knees and petted and cooed in her ears, "Diddle Dee, Sweet Delilah," trying to calm her. I did not oust her from the suitcase until the very last minute, holding her close to me. Then we hid the suitcases in the closest.

We had no idea what the next years would bring. We did know that the precious dogs who brightened our days would have a yard to romp in, and we would have a back porch to sit on and watch them.

Epilogue

Not a day went by that Samson and Delilah did not bring a smile to my face and laughter and joy to our lives. Besides being a delight, they had a wonderful spirit that soared me to greater heights. I was grateful we never abandoned them and put the energy and patience into creating the necessary bonds.

Did they sometimes have a misstep? Of course! Did we wish that things had been easier (whatever that looks like)? No, we realized they were the dogs we were meant to have. They taught us many lessons. Another dog would have just be different—not necessarily better, easier, etc.

A friend recently shared with me a poem entitled *The Touch of the Master's Hand* that tells the story of an old violin that was being auctioned off. The bidding started at $1, then $2, and $3.

An old man walked to the front of the room and picked up the violin and began to play. Beautiful sounds filled the room. When the old man was finished, the auctioneer resumed the bidding.

The bid started at $1,000, then $2,000. Someone asked, "What changed its worth?" Swiftly came the reply, "the touch of the master's hand." It brought the violin to life and gave it worth.

We can all do the same for our children, partners, spouses, and friends. They can be touched with your words, voice, positive attitude about them, and with people by providing respect and dignity.

I sometimes lamented that if I had known what to do sooner, or could have waved a magic wand, Samson and Delilah would have had a happier beginning with less turmoil. But dogs are forgiving. They picked up on the clues, on the changes in my behavior, and responded very quickly. I also have a bullish belief about the spirit of dogs.

In this book you may have found some techniques and strategies, some things to think about, but more importantly there are no easy answers. No one can promise you that if you do one thing, everything will automatically come together.

There is no formula. Every situation is different; every dog unique. Every resolution takes desire. Enjoy the journey and delight in their antics.

Elizabeth

Acknowledgments

What a joy to write this book. What a joy to spend time with Samson and Delilah.

I wish to thank my husband, David, for reading and editing this book, and to Sarah Holler, Joanne Wright, and Sarah Moreno, who were willing readers. I am grateful for all their kindnesses and for inspiring me to get the book published.

Elizabeth has traveled many roads during her life, but the one of writer is most rewarding.

She has authored a book, *Odd Ducks and Birds of a Feather,* to teach personality types based on the work of Swiss psychologist, Carl Jung.

She has also authored a literary novel, *Josephine: A Woman of Indomitable Spirit,* a saga of social injustice that captures the indomitable spirit and tenacity of the women who stood beside their husbands and sons, balanced against the misery of living in a western Pennsylvania coal patch.

www.ingramcontent.com/pod-product-compliance
Lightning Source LLC
Chambersburg PA
CBHW072058290426
44110CB00014B/1736